Nation's
Restaurant News

RESTAU
POCI

COST
CONTROLS

25 KEYS TO

*Profitable
Success*

DAVID V. PAVESIC, F.M.P.

Copyright© 1999 by David V. Pavesic, Ph.D.
Lebhar-Friedman Books

Lebhar-Friedman Books is a company of Lebhar-Friedman Inc.

Printed in the United States of America

Library of Congress Cataloging-in-Publication Data

Pavesic, David V.
    Restaurant manager's pocket handbook : 25 keys to
profitable success. Cost controls / David V. Pavesic.
        p. cm.
    Includes index.
    ISBN 0-86730-751-X (pbk.)
    1. Restaurants--Cost control. I. Title.
TX911.3.C65P386   1998
647.95'0681--dc21   98-39300
                                                          CIP

THE IDEA for the pocket series came to me over the Christmas holidays in 1997 while I was redeeming a gift certificate at Barnes & Noble. Waiting in line to pay for my purchase, I saw stacks of Richard Carlson's book, *Don't Sweat the Small Stuff*, piled up by the check-out registers. It is one of those inspirational-type books that have mass public appeal. I ended up purchasing one.

After I finished reading it, I developed an idea for a supplemental booklet to accompany my recently published book titled, *The Fundamental Principles of Restaurant Cost Control*. I thought, why not put together a small and inexpensive booklet that could be read quickly and easily by restaurant owners and managers that would explain and put into clear perspective the fundamental principles of restaurant cost control?

The principles presented in this book are applicable to any business venture, not just restaurants. Restaurant cost control applies the basic principles of cost accounting, financial analysis, and general management used in any business. I have just applied them to a restaurant. Whatever type of restaurant you own or manage, you will find value in reading this book.

As a college instructor, I have always taught the more quantitative courses that are usually thought to be more difficult than others. They are the most pragmatic and serviceable courses in the program. However, many approach cost control with the same frame of mind they have when going to the dentist. The trepidation that precedes the treatment is more stressful than the actual office procedures. Such it seems is the attitude of owners and managers when it comes to cost controls in their restaurants.

I wrote this book to help operators reduce the anxiety and stress of planning and setting up a cost-control program and as a companion text to *The Fundamental Principles of Restaurant Cost Control.* The latter explains in detail the how and why of the principles that follow in *25 Keys to Profitable Success: Cost Controls.*

25 KEYS TO
COST CONTROLS

Your physical presence is not sufficient for cost control

I REMEMBER MY FATHER telling me the reason he had to work so much in his restaurant. He said that he had to be there to keep the help from stealing from him. Now while I believe that ownership presence in the restaurant sends a positive message to both employees and customers, if you are there for the reason given, you not only are mistaken as to its effectiveness but also are tied to your business and depriving your family of your company.

There are several reasons why your physical presence is insufficient for cost-control purposes. First of all, you cannot see everything that is going on at the same time. When you are in the dining room, you cannot see what is going on in the kitchen. When you are checking in a delivery, you cannot see the cooks preparing the food. You cannot oversee every plate being portioned or every drink being made. You cannot be everywhere at the same time.

In addition, if you feel that your business cannot operate without your being there, you limit your growth and expansion to what you can oversee personally. You will never have more than one location if you think this way. Effective management requires that you delegate responsibility and authority to your subordinates and then let them manage. Yes, they will make some mistakes, but that's the way you learned, from making mistakes. The definition of management is getting things done through people — other people. They may not be able to do it as well as you can. But they can do it.

I have this theory that those who are willing to do a little of everything in the restaurant — sometimes referred to as "jacks of all trades" — have more difficulty delegating than those who know and admit to their limitations. They have to delegate to those who know more than they do about cooking, bartending, or training. When I opened my restaurant, I tried to do everything. I was there all the time.

I had to learn to let go. My brother saw that I was taking things way too seriously and getting stressed out. He suggested I go to the National Restaurant Show in Chicago to get some fresh ideas for our business. Lo and behold, my restaurants were still there when I returned, no worse for my absence. I began to realize I didn't have to be there all the time. That led to our decision to open a second restaurant.

When my brother and partner told me he and his wife were going on a cruise a month before we were to open our second location, I couldn't believe it. We had so much to do. But he was a delegator who trusted and empowered his employees. Unfortunately, I didn't see it that way. I thought it showed irresponsibility and lack of commitment and concern for our business. I was wrong.

Today, our industry still expects its employees to work as if they had no other interests or life outside of work. The restaurant and hotel industry continue to experience high turnover of hourly and managerial employees. We gauge commitment and attitude by how many hours a person works each week, not so much by what he or she accomplishes. I have seen managers boasting that they worked 80 hours last week and have not had a day off in a month. Top management views that like a badge of honor. However, spouses and children never see their husband or wife, father or mother.

In addition to not being able to see everything that ultimately could impact food, labor, or beverage costs, the things you do observe are not telling you the real story. Furthermore, many of the things that negatively impact costs and profits are invisible to the naked eye. This true anecdote was related to me by one of my students writing a cost-control term paper. The California Pizza Kitchen chain can track inventory from menu sales. Whenever an item is sold, the ingredients used are deducted from inventory based on the chain's standardized portions. One end-of-the-month variance report indicated that 25 pounds of mozzarella cheese was missing. Management reviewed the preparation of all menu items using mozzarella, and all it found was a slight overportioning of 0.25

ounce. No one could detect that by watching the pizzas being made. When the 0.25 ounce was multiplied by the total number of pizzas sold during the month, it added up to close to 25 pounds. Without the cost and sales records, it would have taken forever to discover the real cause.

If you are still convinced that spending more time in your restaurant is the only way you can control theft and be certain every dollar of sales is recorded, ask yourself how the major franchise chains monitor franchisees. They don't have supervisors who visit their franchise units and check on their daily operations unless there's a problem. How do franchisors and corporate chains keep tabs on what is going on in the hundreds and even thousands of units across the country and overseas?

The answer is the same way the IRS can tell if a business isn't filing an accurate income tax return. They look at the numbers on various reports and forms that must be filled out. In any business where absentee ownership exists, records are the eyes of the owner — or manager — when he or she is not physically present. The detailed reports on sales by meal period, customer counts, payroll records, purchases, inventory, and menu-sales mix reveal much more than they could ever observe by looking (to paraphrase Yogi Berra). And they don't have to be present to know that sales are underreported — based on purchases and inventory — or that too many employees are scheduled for the volume of business, or that purchases do not match sales levels. The financial and nonfinancial reports are the microscopic eyes of owners and managers.

The menu design, inventory process, and sales-mix analysis are essential elements of cost control

BASICALLY, THE ENTIRE CYCLE of cost controls in a foodservice operation revolves around the central activities of menu design, inventory, and sales analysis. The menu will determine the complexity of your cost controls. A limited menu is easier to control than an extensive menu. You have fewer items to prepare, fewer ingredients to purchase and keep in inventory, and fewer items to keep track of with sales analysis.

Without those three elements your cost controls would not have any validity. The amounts you order, keep in inventory, and prepare are based on what you expect to sell. This is so important you cannot leave it to the memory of your chef or kitchen manager. After all, given the turnover in our industry, you cannot be sure he or she will be around next Easter or

Mother's Day when you need past sales records to help prepare for this year's business.

If you want to know if there is theft, over-portioning, or waste taking place, you need to know how much you started with, how much you had left, and how much you sold. Tracking inventory without comparison to sales does not tell you much. Tracking sales without monitoring quantities prepared is equally incomplete.

Consequently, given the importance of the menu in the overall success and profitability of the restaurant, it must be accorded the same attention as your most-expensive capital expenditure. A well-designed menu is critical if a restaurant expects to achieve its desired check average, gross profit, food cost, and overall sales. In order to purchase, prepare, and staff correctly, management must forecast business levels and know how much of each menu item to prepare. Accurate forecasts of sales cannot be made without historical records. That is why tracking sales, customer counts, and menu popularity is so important.

As for inventory records, knowing what to purchase, from whom, and at what price are important cost considerations. How much to purchase is also critical in cost control. You do not want to run out of product, nor do you want to tie up precious cash in perishable food. Without those three elements cost controls will not be accurate and useful to owners and managers. All other activities ranging from the initial purchasing to paying the accounts after the food has been prepared and served revolve around those functions.

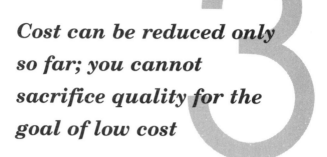

Cost can be reduced only so far; you cannot sacrifice quality for the goal of low cost

KEY 3

SOME OPERATORS BECOME OBSESSED with a cost-control mentality to the point where they lose track of the other aspects of running a successful business. Paying close attention to the supply side of your business will pay off in lower unit costs and increased worker productivity. But opportunities and ideas to drive incremental growth eventually will cease. Resist becoming entirely focused on just achieving the lowest costs; you eventually will have to focus on the TOP line. I must admit that I was brought up to believe that you should always shop for the lowest price, try to utilize everything you buy, and not throw anything away if you can help it. That was reinforced by one of my college professors at Florida State who told us, "Never give away for free what you are in business to sell." By that he meant do not give free drinks

> **"In the final analysis, you cannot continue to reduce costs and grow."**
>
> — Paul Cook

---

or meals to customers.

That stuck in my mind to the point that I was reluctant to "comp" meals for even family and friends. It was reinforced when my restaurateur stepfather declared that he did not like the employees to see him take food home because he would never allow them to do it. I recall a conversation with a restaurant colleague in which we were reminiscing about the "good old days" when we did not comp meals when customers complained; we didn't have to. The cost-control mentality kept us from doing so. We ignored the other side of the transaction — repeat business. When a customer complained about the food, we would apologize but still charge him for his meal.

I also remember using the lettuce that was beginning to get a little brown around the edges because I did not want to throw it away. I even might have said: "Put it out. We'll change it if the a customer says something." Taken to the extreme, there are horror stories of operators and suppliers who have tried to use and sell food that should have been discarded. A report out of Florida even told of a seafood supplier who washed spoiled shrimp in chlorine to remove the fishy smell so he could sell them.

Those are worst-case examples. More often operators shop to obtain the lowest price from a supplier without regard for quality or consistency. The cheapest frozen french fry or mayonnaise will not have the quality of a branded product. Buying only on the basis of price will result in poor quality and usually more waste.

The same is true when it comes to scheduling employees and the prevailing wage rate you pay them. You can keep you payroll costs down by paying minimum wage and scheduling too few employees. In the long run the quality of service and employee morale will decrease. The old saw that says, "You get what you pay for," should be remembered. The exhilaration of paying a cheap price quickly dissipates upon realizing that you have purchased substandard quality. In addition, you probably lost a customer or two in the process.

Low cost cannot be the single-minded goal of cost control. You must temper that by saying, "The lowest cost *consistent with quality standards for food and service.*" If you do not provide value to the customer, if you do not pay your more productive employees a premium, if customers do not receive good service, then achieving low costs will not result in financial success.

Ironically, if you want to be known for quality food and service, you'll need to spend more than the average operator to achieve it. You'll have to train your employees on the nuances of quality service. It doesn't come naturally. Quality ingredients and productive employees cost more than the average quality ingredients and workers. In addition, many businesses with adequate cost controls still go out of business. The reason is lack of sales revenue. The causes of low sales may be any number of things, such as low quality, small portions, high prices, poor service, bad location, or competition, to name a few.

The point is that your total business strategy requires more than just a cost-control component. Once costs have been reduced to the minimum — without sacrificing standards of quality — they can go no lower. Then the strategy must switch to a marketing perspective to increase customer traffic and overall sales revenue.

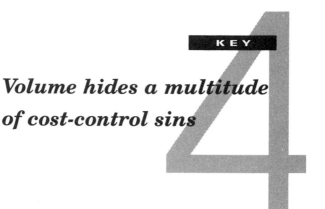

Volume hides a multitude of cost-control sins

IT'S MUCH EASIER TO MAKE a profit in a high-volume operation than in one with a low sales volume. Once you are over the break-even point, every additional dollar of sales contributes a greater percentage to your bottom-line profit. When business is below or just above break-even, waste and lost sales impact costs and profits noticeably. I've known several young men and women who, after managing a high-volume casual-theme restaurant, feel they were ready to go into business for themselves. I told them that the fact that their operation is doing $3.5 million hides many of the cost inefficiencies that would be noticeable if the operation were doing only $1.5 million.

Houston's Restaurants is a great example of how high volume contributes to management's ability to maintain high food-quality

> **"Never say no when a client asks for something, even if it is the moon. You can always try, and anyhow there is plenty of time afterwards to explain that it was not possible."**
>
> — CESAR RITZ

---

standards. Managers are required to do taste plates at every meal period, and their quality-control standards are such that food that doesn't meet standards is discarded. Over a month's time that quality-control waste could amount to hundreds of dollars. In most restaurants that could amount to at least 1 percent of food sales and be a major cause of concern. However, a typical Houston's restaurant will average in a week what another might do in a month. As a result, the known waste amounts to less than 0.25 percent. In fact, if district managers don't see quality-control waste on kitchen reports, they will question whether the quality standards are being met.

Contrast that with to the operation that is only marginally profitable and one in which every dollar of waste is felt. It's harder to maintain high quality standards in those operations, and management is more likely to use marginal items rather than to throw them out. One simple piece of advice that I pass on to owners and managers is: "When in doubt, throw it out." An employee — whether manager, cook, or server — is not likely to be reprimanded for not serving a marginal item; however, an employee may lose his or her job by serving food that results in a customer complaint.

With competition as stiff as it is today, no restaurant can expect to win repeat business from a customer who had to pay for something he or she did not like or found unsatisfactory. An increasing number of restaurants are adopting service guarantees. If for any reason a customer is not happy with the food or service, she is not charged. In fact, some operators will go one step further and give the customer a gift certificate for the next meal at no charge.

That is a necessary strategy today. It is critical to build quality-control costs into your pricing structure so managers will comp meals willingly to customers who received less than the standard of food quality and service you aim to provide. You must have a marketing strategy to optimize your sales volume; you cannot rely on low costs to build sales volume. It comes from providing price-value to the customer, giving great service, and serving quality foods in a clean and inviting environment.

(1) The most effective way to manage is to:
- A. Do everything yourself
- B. Delegate noncritical responsibility to employees, but monitor them closely
- C. Delegate responsibility and authority to others and allow them to make their own mistakes

(2) A good manager can personally observe everything that may impact costs and profits negatively.
- A. True
- B. False

(3) Which of the following is not an essential element of food cost control?
- A. Inventory process
- B. Menu design
- C. Hiring and firing
- D. Sales-mix analysis

(4) A restaurant will almost always succeed if its management remains focused on achieving the lowest costs.
- A. True
- B. False

(5) A high-volume operation can hide many cost inefficiencies.
- A. True
- B. False

ANSWERS: 1: C, 2: B, 3: C, 4: B, 5: A

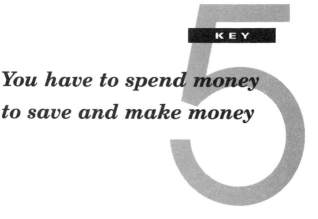

You have to spend money to save and make money

THAT MAY AT FIRST SEEM CONTRADICTORY to cost control, but it's not. It hearkens back to what was mentioned earlier about the fallacy of just trying to adopt a strategy of cost containment at the expense of food and service quality. In order to serve quality food, you must use quality ingredients — and, not surprising, they cost more than lower quality ingredients.

By the same token, if you want to attract the best employees to prepare and serve the food, you need to pay them more than the competition does. If you want them to uphold your service standards, you will have to train them so they understand and are able to execute those standards. Don't make the mistake of thinking that they will develop your standards on their own. You need to keep these employees longer because you have invested money in

> **" Motivate them, train them, care about them and make winners out of them. We know that if we treat our employees correctly, they'll treat the customers right. And if customers are treated right, they'll come back. "**
>
> — J. Willard Marriott Jr.

---

their training. That means you have to maintain a work environment that demonstrates to the employees that you value their effort and contribution to your business.

Furthermore, you have to spend money to provide management and employees with the latest equipment and utensils so they can be more productive. And you need to keep your dining room, kitchen, and parking lot clean and safe for both customers and employees.

Those things cost money. If you are not willing to compensate your employees in a way that demonstrates how much you value them, or spend the money necessary for training them, or see that they have the equipment and resources necessary to allow them to do their jobs efficiently, you will not be able to sustain your competitive edge in the marketplace.

I am reminded of the top-selling business

book of the 1980s, *In Search of Excellence*, by Peters and Waterman, in which the authors reported that cost and efficiency, over the long run, follow from an emphasis on quality, customer service, innovation, participation, and a customer-focused philosophy. The companies that paid attention to their customers and employees not only achieved but also exceeded their financial goals. Volume hides a multitude of cost-control sins, and attention to quality brings about higher sales volume.

Cost-control programs have a cost to them, whether the components be electronic, mechanical, or manual. They also include a time component for which management must assemble, organize, and analyze the reports and schedules. Computers have compressed the time it takes to record and organize the kind of data management needed to control cost. Because of the development of computer software programs for cost-control purposes, management now spends the majority of its time analyzing the data instead of compiling the reports.

So it would seem that quality standards and the willingness to invest in cost controls work hand in hand. Once you have raised your volume above the break-even point, you will become more comfortable with your quality-control standards and be more willing to invest time and money in your cost-control program.

(1) An increasing number of restaurants are adopting:

    A. Dress codes for staff members
    B. Service guarantees
    C. Mission statements
    D. All of the above

(2) A restaurateur can always rely on low costs to build sales volume.

    A. True
    B. False

(3) In order to serve quality food, you must:

    A. Purchase imported items
    B. Hire an expensive kitchen staff
    C. Use quality ingredients

(4) Good employees should be:

    A. Be paid above average compensation
    B. Recognized for their efforts
    C. Trained well
    D. All of the above
    E. None of the above

(5) Quality standards and the willingness to invest in cost controls work hand in hand.

    A. True
    B. False

ANSWERS: 1: D, 2: B, 3: C, 4: D, 5: A

KEY

Cost controls are first and foremost preventive, not corrective

A KEY ASPECT OF COST CONTROL is the prevention of the cost excess in the first place rather than having to take a corrective action after the loss has been discovered. Another way of putting it is that the goal is to maximize profits, not to minimize losses. Think about it. Who would want to have as a goal the task of minimizing losses? Unfortunately, a number of operators turn to cost controls when losses are occurring and the damage has been done already.

Cost controls are not just for operators who need to reduce their costs. They're needed in those successful high-volume operations where volume hides a multitude of sins. A significant opportunity exists to maximize profits when the business volume is there. A business may be lulled into thinking that it's doing fine because a profit is being shown. However, that

> **"The will to win is not nearly as important as the will to prepare to win."**
>
> — ANONYMOUS

---

business never will know how much additional profit could have been made if excess costs were controlled.

You must put your cost-control program into effect the first day you open the doors — although it actually begins when you start incurring expenses for the planning and development of the concept. Converting to a cost-control program when the business has been losing money often comes too late to turn things around. Remember: Cost controls in and of themselves are not a guaranteed formula for financial success. You must have the entire package in place to be successful today.

We have all read that businesses that pay attention to quality also seem to do other things right, and costs generally fall in line. But the opposite is also true. Those businesses whose costs are excessive and out of line presumably are not doing the other things necessary to make their business successful. When food and service quality is suspect, sales volume likely will suffer as well.

I recall something one of my professors said in a principles of management class many years ago about "putting out fires." If management spends too much time trying to put out the same fires over and over — a synonym for what is called "crisis management" — it most likely has not addressed the cause of those problems and is simply reacting to the symptoms. Such is the case with management always correcting costs after it has exceeded standards.

Think of your cost-control program as a casualty insurance policy for your business — fire protection, for example. Your insurance company will charge you a premium based on the likelihood of a loss occurring and the amount of damages that would result. Remember the television ads on the old *Zoo Parade* with Marlin Perkins, in which the Mutual of Omaha stag would be shown walking through the plant or factory? Did you ever catch the symbolism of the stag in the factory? What it meant was that Mutual of Omaha was going to help its clients minimize the possibility that a loss would even occur in the first place. What the company offered as a service was that its loss underwriters would inspect your facility and report back any conditions that were unsafe. If you made the necessary repairs, your premium was lowered. That is called loss prevention. Think of your cost-control program in the same way.

(1) As the use of computers becomes more widespread, operators now must spend more time compiling reports.

    A. True
    B. False

(2) Cost control should be preventative, not corrective.

    A. True
    B. False

(3) A business is successful as long as a profit is being shown.

    A. True
    B. False

(4) Ideally, a cost-control program should be put into effect:

    A. Within a month of opening
    B. One week after opening
    C. The day you open
    D. As soon as you begin incurring expenses for planning and development

(5) If management has to put out the same fires repeatedly, it is doing its job.

    A. True
    B. False

ANSWERS: 1: B, 2: A, 3: B, 4: D, 5: B

Cost controls are more often proactive than they are reactive

THAT FUNDAMENTAL PREMISE follows the previous one and basically states that cost controls are preemptive measures that imply advance planning. It is a little like the naval damage-control officer who is charged with mitigating the losses that the ship might suffer when it goes into action. The ship may take a shell or torpedo, so the job of damage control is to make repairs as soon as possible.

Cost controls are primarily proactive measures established to keep costs in line with standards and allow the operation to maximize its profits. The sooner cost inefficiencies are discovered, the sooner financial damage can be corrected. Consequently, we have to watch the little things like portion control, purchase prices, inventory levels, guest-check controls, employee schedules, linen costs, utilities, and supplies expenses. If we can catch the cost leaks when they are small, we can reduce potential losses before they become serious.

If we do not have a reporting system to detect the variances that we cannot see with our eyes — or a way of measuring the long-term effects of those we can see — costs may drift way out of line before we are able to do anything about them. If you are moved to respond only in a reactive manner, you are not in control of your operation.

Cost controls are not just for detecting dishonesty

THE PREVENTION AND DETECTION of fraud and theft are just ancillary benefits of a cost-control program, a premise that is not always clear to independent operators. After I conducted several discussions with independent restaurateurs about the need for cost controls, they would tell me that they now understood the true purpose and value of cost controls. A few independent owners felt that their physical presence and the hiring of family members eliminated the need for cost controls. Once they progressed beyond the singular idea that cost controls are to keep people from stealing and understood that the primary purpose was to provide feedback on day-to-day operations and decisions, they appreciated the real purpose and value.

Why don't all restaurant operators have cost-control programs? The answer is that they are not aware of the waste that is taking place around them. It is not very complicated, as it is all basic management. You have to be able to identify value, and you have to know your costs and detect where they are excessive. Cost control encompasses all areas — from the back door to the front door; from purchasing to paying your bills; from recording each transaction to depositing the sales receipts in the bank. Cost control is also more than just computing percentages and ratios; it involves making decisions after the information has been compiled and interpreted.

Cost control is used to monitor the efficiency of individuals and departments; to inform management of what expenses are being incurred and what incomes are being received; and whether they are within standards or budgets. In essence, cost controls are for knowing where the business is headed, not for discovering where it has been. That enforces the preventative and proactive purposes of cost controls.

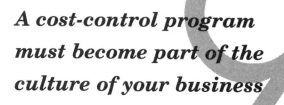

A cost-control program must become part of the culture of your business

TO PARAPHRASE National Restaurant Association chief executive Herman Cain, "A cost-control program is a journey, not a destination." In fact, describing it as a program does not properly put it into perspective because the term implies something that is only temporary. However, cost controls are not temporary or a response to hard times.

I can think back to when I first went to work as a busboy in one of my stepfather's restaurants and how my perspective has changed regarding cost control. I thought that his managing partner was the most cost-conscious person I had ever met — an initial opinion I reached because he never let us throw anything away. We were instructed to recycle vegetables that were not touched by the guests — that was a judgment call — and we kept bread from the

> **"I have found that being honest is the best technique I can use. Right up front, tell people what you're trying to accomplish and what you're willing to sacrifice to accomplish it."**
>
> — LEE IACOCCA

---

table to make bread crumbs.

After I started taking classes in restaurant management at Florida State, I came to realize that those examples not only were unsanitary but also were not the way to control food costs. However, that restaurant had a "culture" — one of thrift and controlling waste. And that needs to be the attitude of all employees regarding cost controls. That lesson must be instilled in everyone: in the dishwasher who handles expensive china, silver, and glassware; in the busboy pouring water, replenishing butter, and clearing tables; in the kitchen worker peeling onions and garlic; in the bartender mixing drinks; in the server setting tables and receiving payment from customers.

If an operation practices cost control in all of its activities, the costs of operation will be lower than that of the competition. Profits will be above average even if the operation charges the same prices as the restaurant down the street. In fact, it could even charge lower prices than the competition and still make as much or more profit. Imagine the competitive advantage if your prices were lower and the quality of your food and service was equal to or better than that of your rivals.

Cost control needs to be ingrained into the culture of your restaurant. When such a business philosophy becomes ingrained, it is said to be "institutionalized." It is critical that your staff place a premium on absolutely, positively getting the greatest value for the least cost in every aspect of your operation. Some managers and owners hide facts and figures from their employees out of fear that if they know the restaurant is losing money, they will start looking for another job — or, conversely, if they know a profit is being earned, they will lobby for raises.

Your employees should be told what it costs to operate the restaurant. You would be amazed at the misconceptions that employees have on profit. More often than not, they will overstate the profit on a menu item. Show employees how their performance affects the overall profitability of the restaurant. Use examples of how waste, overportioning, overtime, theft, and breakage affects overall profitability.

Once cost controls have become institutionalized in your business, employees will identify with ownership interests and adopt a more conscious approach toward waste and inefficiency. Quality control is the responsibility of both the individual employee and management. Service and cost standards must be self-monitored because management cannot over-see every transaction and employee-customer encounter. The internalization of the cost and quality mentality is not accomplished by substi-tuting rules for judgment. Judgment can be developed only by empowering your employ-ees and trusting that they will respond with your interests in serving the customer.

10

Standards, both qualitative and quantitative, are essential elements of any cost-control program

SETTING STANDARDS IS AN INTEGRAL PART of any cost-control program. Standards are measures that establish a value for comparison by first establishing minimum acceptable results. Those values become the yardsticks with which management sets qualitative and quantitative levels of performance for individuals and operating results. Actual results are evaluated by comparison with standards to determine if they meet, exceed, or fall below expectations. Your standards must reflect elements of both quality and quantity and contribute to achieving your profit goals.

When comparing actual results with standards, the difference between resources planned and the resources used is the variance from the standard. When a positive variance occurs — that is, when performance exceeds the standard — management should praise or

> **"**Standards are more than 'conforming to requirements' or hitting or exceeding a benchmark. It is also more than 'delighting' or 'wowing.' It is doing something so well that you are the *only* one who does what you do.**"**

> — TOM PETERS

---

reward those responsible. If a negative variance occurs, those responsible should be held accountable. And while standards can reveal where individuals or entire departments have or have not met standards, they also can serve as preventive measures that reduce or eliminate how often corrective action must be taken.

While it is recommended that you establish your standards in writing, that is not the determining factor that makes it a formal standard. Many independent operators maintain consistent standards without writing a word. The day-to-day practices of management become internalized and a standard of performance is implicit in the culture. It is therefore not what is written, but rather what is practiced that defines a formal standard. I learned early in my management career that it worked better to start off being strict and then eventually ease up than the other way around. If you start off being too lenient, it becomes extremely difficult, if not impossible, to bring recalcitrant employees in line because they will not take you seriously.

Standards become part of the philosophy and culture of the business. That occurs only when employees are thoroughly committed to the values of the business. Management must set the standards; you cannot expect or allow employees to set qualitative or quantitative standards. Nor can you adopt the standards of another restaurant company and expect to achieve the same results. Each operation must establish its own standards relative to its financial idiosyncrasies and position in the marketplace. That is necessary since all of the variables that will influence cost standards differ from operation to operation — even within a chain of fast-food restaurants. Rent, property taxes, interest rates, debt-equity ratio, depreciation schedules, land costs, and the like all affect the cost and profit standards that will be acceptable.

National chains have come to realize that they cannot establish a single standard for any cost that will be applicable to any given location. Cost standards must be determined from observations and calculations occurring under actual operating conditions, not as the result of some unrealistic and highly controlled tests conducted in laboratorylike conditions. The danger is that standards arrived at through unrealistic test circumstances actually will understate costs.

I have a favorite saying regarding management expectations and standards of performance: "A person will deviate from prescribed standards just as far as management allows." That applies to our personal lives in that we have tested our parents' standards. And if you have children, you will recall that they tested yours in turn. When told to be home by a certain hour, a child will test us to determine "just how late he or she can be" and still not get into trouble. Is it five minutes, or is it 30 minutes? Such is the case with employees.

Now having said that, I need to include a disclaimer on standards. While having standards is critically important when it comes to the quality of your products and services, the pursuit of perfection may be to the detriment of your overall success. C. Northcote Parkinson, of Parkinson's Law fame, said, "Perfection is achieved only by institutions on the point of collapse." I take that to mean that we can never be completely satisfied with what we are doing. We need to adopt a "best-I-ever-made" attitude every time we do or make something. When we are finished we must be able to say, "This is even better than the last time, but I think we can still do better."

Wealth flows from innovations, not from optimization — not by perfecting the known, but by imperfectly seizing the unknown. That attitude is necessary because this is the age of the never-satisfied customer. While our standards are high and we may achieve consistency, we also may become increasingly ordinary in the eyes of the consumer. Setting and maintaining standards has to be more than just meeting or exceeding benchmarks; we need to surprise and wow the customer.

Your cost-control program is only as strong as its weakest component

EFFECTIVE COST-CONTROL SYSTEMS must start at the top of the organization. No control program can function well unless ownership and management are committed to enforcing the standards and procedures. Central to every restaurant operation are what I refer to as the 12 primary functions. Visualize those 12 functions as if they were planets revolving around the sun and the sun represents the menu, sales analysis, and inventory records.

Remember: It is the menu that drives the control process and determines what the customer will buy, the specifications for the items purchased, and the quantities held in inventory. The primary functions that exist in each restaurant operation cover every activity from the deliveries at the back entrance to deposits in your bank account. The 12 functions are pur-

> **" The only difference between stumbling blocks and stepping stones is the way you use them."**
>
> — ANONYMOUS

chasing, receiving, storage, issuing, pre-preparation (rough prep), preparation (for service), portioning, transfer of food from kitchen to dining room, order taking/guest check, cash receipts, bank deposits, and accounts payable.

Many of the functions overlap and are simultaneously performed. All are interrelated and must be monitored, or you never will uncover the real cause of any variance between actual and standard costs. Controls for each function must be operative as soon as the personnel are assigned or have access to the function area. Another way to look at the 12 function areas is to imagine each function as one link in a chain. That chain will only be as strong as the weakest link.

Such is the case with your cost-control program. Some managers and owners are good at controlling costs in one or two of the function areas but less attentive to the others. That can leave many holes for losses to occur and go undetected until they become extensive. The function areas can be separated into two categories: front-of-the-house (the dining area) and back-of-the-house (kitchen, storage, etc.).

If the cost-control effort is focused on the kitchen and neglected in the dining room, financial goals still may not be attained. Worse yet, unwarranted pressure could be placed on individuals and function areas that are not at fault. Closely monitoring recipes, waste, and portioning is useless when customers are not charged for food served or when sales go unreported.

The information gathered for cost-control purposes is used by many different individuals and function areas. For example, sales-analysis data such as customer counts and menu-item popularity help the dining room manager schedule servers and bus help. The same information can be employed by the buyer who needs to know what and how much to purchase and keep in inventory. It also is used by the kitchen manager to determine quantities to prepare. In addition, management interprets the information to schedule advertising promotions and to evaluate actual results to standards and budgets.

That kind of information can be interpreted only from internal records and reports. You cannot expect to monitor all 12 function areas with your physical presence. Cost and sales records are your "eyes." Records are a critical element of cost controls.

(1) If you are always on the premises or a relative is watching your operation, you really don't need to worry about developing a cost-control program.

    A. True
    B. False

(2) Employees should be allowed to set the standards for an operation.

    A. True
    B. False

(3) Which of the following elements affect cost and profit standards?

    A. Property taxes
    B. Land costs
    C. Debt-equity ratio
    D. All of the above
    E. None of the above

(4) Which of the following is not one of the 12 primary functions of restaurant operations?

    A. Site selection
    B. Purchasing
    C. Receiving
    D. Preparation
    E. Accounts payable

(5) The two major function areas for controlling costs are front- and back-of-the-house.

    A. True
    B. False

ANSWERS: 1: B, 2: B, 3: D, 4: A, 5: A

Cost control is the recording and analysis of financial and operational data. Cost reduction is the action taken to keep cost contained

COST CONTROL IS MORE than just computing percentages and ratios. It involves making decisions after the information has been compiled and interpreted. Terms like "cost accounting" and "bookkeeping" are not cost controls, but the means of gathering the information necessary for cost control to take place.

The word "control" does not have a particularly friendly connotation when it is applied to individuals. It implies restrictions and limits. A dictionary definition refers to it as "a process or function that is used to regulate, verify, or check that which is accomplished through some method, device, or system." Control means to exercise authority and to restrain. Control is placed over all items of income and expense. However, most of the effort is given to controlling food, beverage, and labor. There is

> **"It sounds extraordinary, but it's a fact that balance sheets can make fascinating reading."**
>
> — MARY ARCHER

very good reason that these three costs are given the most attention. Consider that the capital costs of building, land, and equipment could exceed $4 million or $5 million. But over the life of a restaurant, more will be spent on food, beverage, and labor.

There is no way around it: Cost control is a numbers game. At first glance, paying attention to numbers is viewed as a job for an accountant, a controller, or a financial consultant. It involves accounting, a process that is routine drudgery to most of us. However, if you want a detailed assessment of what's going on in your restaurant, you need numbers — lots of them. The numbers you collect must be organized, interpreted, and compared. Those numbers may represent what happened during a particular meal period, day, week, month, or year.

The interpretation of the numbers is something you cannot delegate. You have to do it yourself so that you can tell others what's going on without having to wait for someone to tell you that a problem exists. The numbers are your controls. You do not have to be present while the restaurant is open to know that food and labor costs are out of line. The numbers will tell you. Comprehension of the numbers comes only with constant review, an understanding of what they should be, and knowing the relationship between expenses and revenues.

Eventually, you will find yourself looking forward to preparing cost reports and reviewing the numbers. The ratios and percentages you calculate will reveal the information you need to assess the effectiveness of your decisions and whether standards are being upheld. Knowing what happened in the past can provide insight into what is likely to happen in the future. Understanding the numbers puts you in control.

Once you have mastered the numbers, you are no longer reading just numbers any more than you are reading just words in this book. You are reading meanings! Your eyes will see numbers, but your mind will be reading the stories behind the numbers — labor productivity, portion control, inventory levels, purchase prices, marketing promotions, new menu items, and competitive strategy.

Cost control is more than the accumulation and interpretation of information, filling out schedules and reports, taking inventory, costing out recipes, and computing percentages and ratios. It moves to the next step of taking the necessary action to keep costs and standards in line to maintain profitability. The control aspect is accomplished through the compilation, assembly, and interpretation of cost data. Our knowledge of the numbers tells us what happened and why. Cost *reduction* is the actual changing of the factors that will influence food, beverage, and labor cost in some positive way, usually lowering the percentage. Cost *reduction* is the action taken to bring costs within accepted standards — that is, preportioning ingredients prior to final preparation; following standardized recipes; employing measuring devices to portion items; using dispensing systems and scales to measure and weigh portions.

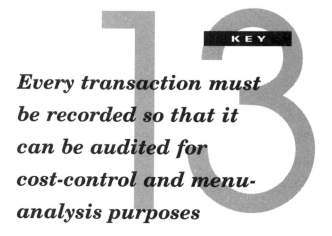

Every transaction must be recorded so that it can be audited for cost-control and menu-analysis purposes

THE IMPORTANCE OF RECORDING every transaction is critically important to the cost-control and menu-analysis function. If food or beverage can be requisitioned by servers without having the transaction documented in some way, you will never know the extent to which items are being stolen, given away, or sold to paying customers. In order to get food from the kitchen or beverages from the bar, the transaction needs to be manually recorded on a serially numbered guest check or entered into a point-of-sale computer system.

Cooks and bartenders should be instructed not to fill any order unless they have a printed check for those items. That includes such non-cash transactions as employee and management meals. No one, including management, is exempt from the policy. If printed guest checks

> **"Your biggest expense is the money you don't make."**
>
> — PANTE

are used, they need to be serially numbered and signed out to specific servers. Missing checks must be detected every meal period. If a mistake or void occurs, it must be initialed by a member of management.

Once the transaction is recorded and entered, it can be audited by management for cost-control purposes. You must compare the number of items sold with the amount purchased and remaining in inventory to determine whether theft, waste, or overportioning is occurring. Sales information also is necessary to determine preparation quantities and par inventory levels. And the recording of each transaction is important for menu-sales analysis purposes. You need to know which items are selling and how the sales mix impacts your overall food cost, average check, sales revenue, and gross profit.

You don't necessarily require an expensive point-of-sale system to record each transaction. The duplicate check system continues to be employed today in many restaurants and is still effective if used correctly. Kitchen and bar copies, called the "soft" check, are matched with the "hard" guest check to ensure that all items requisitioned from the kitchen and bar have been recorded.

If a point-of-sale system is used, all orders "sent" to the kitchen or bar are "locked" in the system. Changes cannot be made without management overrides. However, both systems are only as good as management requires them to be. If servers can get food and drink by verbal orders or make verbal alterations that impact the sales mix or food and beverage cost, the chain of control is broken. That is perhaps the most important element of your cost-control program. You need to be certain that all transactions are entered into the system so that they can be tracked.

(1) Cost accounting and bookkeeping are cost controls.
  A. True
  B. False

(2) Over the life of a restaurant, an operator will spend the most on:
  A. Building, land, and equipment
  B. Food, beverage, and labor

(3) Cost reduction is the actual changing of the factors that will influence food, beverage, and labor cost in some positive way.
  A. True
  B. False

(4) Printed guest checks should:
  A. Be available in several colors
  B. Be serially numbered and signed out to specific servers
  C. Have two carbons

(5) Servers should be allowed to get certain food items or beverages through verbal orders.
  A. True
  B. False

ANSWERS: 1: B, 2: B, 3: A, 4: B, 5: B

The days of the strict bean-counter mentality are over

GIVEN THE ABUNDANCE OF TALENT in the restaurant industry today, an independent operator sees the challenge of competing against the national chains as the equivalent of leaping the Grand Canyon. An old Chinese proverb states, "You don't leap a chasm in two bounds." Neither do you gain ground — or even hold on to what you already have — by following a policy of incremental cost reductions, the preferred strategy of the "bean-counter." Simply speaking, you cannot continue to reduce costs and grow your business.

I was taught that if you concentrated on saving the nickels and dimes, your profits would improve in dollars. The image of the cost-conscious manager with the personality of Ebenezer Scrooge comes to mind with the term bean-counter. A philosophy designed to squeeze every penny out of every dollar spent and force every ounce of productivity from every employee is innovation's worst enemy.

If you're spending all of your time trying to save those nickels and dimes by improving upon what you did yesterday, you become a vulnerable target for your competition. Trying to achieve perfection and zero defects may have you refining yesterday's paradigm at the expense of developing new products and services and exploring other markets that will grow your top line.

Today, such a lopsided perspective to running a business — especially one in which the consumer is so intimately involved — would undoubtedly fail miserably. Revenue enhancement through new products, new services, and delivery of them to the customer must be a large part of your business plan. You cannot wait for evolution to bring about change; it takes too long. You need to have impatient executives and managers who understand the urgency of acting quickly and running counter to the bean-counter mentality.

The role of yesterday's manager as a steward or conservator is no longer an effective use of time and talent. Today, innovation through value-added projects and new ideas is what the business requires.

In the not-too-distant past, management tended to shy away from new and different approaches — particularly if they ran counter to established "boiler-plate" policies and procedures. I have always wondered why Kentucky Fried Chicken wasn't the first company to introduce crispy and spicy varieties of chicken. With that in mind, I offer the following hypothetical tale, circa 1968. Suppose for a moment that a young and enthusiastic executive, manager, or franchisee of the Kentucky Fried Chicken chain approaches the board of that the company and suggests that they introduce a crispy variety to complement the Colonel's Original chicken.

At this time KFC is the largest retailer of cooked chicken in the world and the leading chicken restaurant in the country. Now, if those executives are thinking like stewards and con-servators, they almost certainly would reject the idea instantly. Such a suggestion would border on blasphemy. After all, wasn't it the Original KFC that had made the company so successful? Any variation on that product would have to be a completely crazy idea that cannot possibly fit the image of the brand as management might view it at that point in time.

If such a conversation ever took place — and I seriously doubt it did — I wonder what the person who had the idea might have done. Maybe he or she would have gone to a com-petitor, who decided to try it. Or perhaps a new chicken chain would be developed based on the idea. What the executives in this fabricated tale didn't remember was that when Harland Sanders first introduced the KFC product, his special spices and cooking method most likely were received by many as being crazy, too. But someone had to break with tradition, take a chance, and assume the risk of failing.

I wonder what Dave Thomas of Wendy's was told by his colleagues when he described his idea about an old-fashioned hamburger to compete with McDonald's. I am sure at least one person told him he was crazy and wasting his time and money. Ray Kroc also was considered crazy when he first presented his plan for McDonald's. He had a difficult time finding suppliers who would carry the quantities and products he specified. Managers with years of experience and education hold on to old theories and ideas to the point that it suffocates innovative thinking.

If you find yourself rejecting a new idea because you have never heard of it, or because you tried it once and it didn't work, or because "we have always done it another way," you may be stifling innovation and growth in your company. I remember how my stepfather, an independent restaurateur, scoffed at McDonald's when it was getting started because the idea of a 15-cent hamburger went against his definition of a "good" hamburger.

I wonder where Christianity would be today if Jesus waited for a consensus before he said or did what he felt he had to do. A leader cannot wait for a consensus. Bold decisions will make some people angry. If people don't call some of your decisions crazy, you are probably managing the status quo. The top line grows from innovations, not from being preoccupied with bean counting.

It is absolutely necessary to take a monthly fiscal inventory of food, beverages, and supplies

I AM AMAZED whenever I hear that a restaurant does not take a fiscal inventory every month. By fiscal inventory I mean counting what is on-hand at the end of the month and extending the value. In order for the monthly income statement to reflect accurately the cost of food consumed and sold, you must take a complete food inventory. There is no substitute or shortcut for taking a fiscal count of food, beverages, and supplies if you expect your cost ratios and percentage to show what actually is taking place in your restaurant.

I look for two things when examining the monthly income statements of a restaurant that will tell me if management is computing food and beverage cost percentages accurately. One is whether there is a line-expense item for employee meals on the income statement. The other is found — or not found — in the current-asset section of the balance sheet. Each statement should include a dollar amount that represents the unused inventory of food, alcoholic beverages, and supplies — this is, china, silver, glassware, etc. Remember: Inventory is an asset until it is consumed.

If those entries are missing, the financial information provided by the income statement is suspect. Ask yourself how the operation arrives at the figure for food-cost expense shown on the income statement. It may be the total of the purchases for the month. Depending upon how much an operation keeps in inventory, purchases could either overstate or understate the true cost of goods consumed during the accounting period. One restaurant operator told me that he took a fiscal count with price extensions only at the end of the business year. For 11 months the financial reports and bottom-line profit or loss are inaccurate.

When I don't see a separate line expense for employee meals — even when inventory is taken — I know that the food cost probably has been overstated. That is particularly relevant when you provide free or discounted meals to employees. If you provide free meals as part of the total compensation to your employees, you can take a wage credit for the reasonable cost of the food employees consume. Employee meals can amount to as much as 2 percent to 3 percent of your food cost and therefore need to be tracked as a separate cost. You must back out employee meals to arrive at your true cost of food sold.

Inventory is taken more than once a

month. However, it is not a fiscal inventory. You take inventory (count how much is currently in stock) every time you order those items from a supplier. The more frequently you have an item delivered, the more often you will take inventory of that item. Perishables such as produce, fresh meats, and seafood are inventoried more frequently than nonperishable canned and dry goods. In either case a fiscal month-end inventory must be taken as part of your cost-control program.

One operator told me that the reason he did not take inventory every month was that his business volume was extremely steady, and he purchased the same quantities every week. While I find that hard to accept, consider how the amounts you have in inventory will differ depending on the day of week. Typically, you will find more inventory on hand on a Friday in anticipation of the weekend than on a Monday. Even if you accept the premise that purchases are pretty much the same every week, the actual month-end inventory will vary by thousands of dollars depending on the day of the week the month ends. The information that inventory provides on usage levels alone more than justifies the need to review it regularly.

I understand that many managers approach the month-end inventory process with dread and view it as a tedious activity. When that's the case, it's usually because management must remain until the early-morning hours, counting items. However, the highly important activity should not be any more unpleasant than reconciling the sales for the day, making up employee schedules, or paying the monthly bills.

There must be written records listing all goods purchased. The owner or manager who claims to have that information "in his or her head" and shuns written records leaves the operation open to serious problems. In the event of employee illness, transfer, or dismissal, management can turn to written records to determine purchase requirements.

Cost control requires that regular and accurate inventories of food, beverages, and supplies be taken. When it comes to food and beverages, taking inventory prior to placing the order provides management with the "pulse" of the restaurant activity. When you combine the inventory and purchasing information with sales records and customer counts, you develop an important perspective of the business activity that can alert you to serious problems. As an owner-operator, I didn't delegate inventory taking to my assistants. I knew my business so well that I could detect breakage, recipes that were not followed correctly, and errors in deliveries. I compared the information from sales, production, customer counts, and purchases with what I had on hand at any given time.

Without taking time to count the items you have on hand prior to placing an order, one of two problems are likely to occur. First, you may run out of something before the next delivery and be forced to substitute ingredients. That violates your standardized recipe and changes the raw food cost. The other problem is having too much on hand and tying up needed capital in perishable food products. You take up valuable space and increase the likelihood of spoilage and theft.

A restaurant's menu is its most important cost-control tool

THE NUCLEUS OF ANY FOODSERVICE operation is its menu. The menu is a restaurant's ultimate controlling factor and functions as its profit center, customer-attractor, and theme-determinant. It's an oversimplification to consider the menu to be a mere list of food items offered by a restaurant. A menu must also be judged on its potential for impacting the revenue and operational efficiency of an establishment.

A well-designed menu can make things a lot easier for the operator. It can help keep costs in line and even help distribute the workload in the kitchen. A menu can be designed to influence the amount a customer will spend and generate the check average needed to achieve daily sales projections based on seating, customer counts, and hours of operation. Being able to "guide" a customer's selection will

> **"If one does not know to which port one is sailing, no wind is favorable."**
>
> — SENECA

improve the accuracy of sales forecasts, purchases, preparation quantities, and even labor scheduling.

The product and worker flow in the kitchen will be driven largely by the menu-sales mix. A menu will dictate the skill levels of the employees in both the kitchen and the dining room. The information the menu provides will help management select specific equipment and the best way in which to arrange that equipment for efficiency of production.

The popularity and price of each menu item will impact the amount spent by your customers — and, as a result, influence the average check and daily sales. Furthermore, the sales mix will determine what the overall food cost will be. If it becomes necessary to reduce food cost, management must change one or more of the following elements:

(1) The menu price.
(2) The portion size or number of accompaniments.
(3) The food cost of the ingredients.
(4) The menu mix.

Simply stated, you can raise or discount prices; increase or decrease portion sizes or accompaniments; shop for better ingredient prices; or attempt to alter the sales mix by emphasizing higher-priced or lower-cost menu items through internal advertising and suggestive selling.

A properly designed menu can direct the attention of the diner to specific items and increase the likelihood that those items will be ordered more frequently than random chance consideration. When those items are low in food cost, high in gross profit, and increase the average check, the profit picture brightens and the food cost improves. The menu clearly does have a significant impact on food cost, and if used properly it can be an important cost-control tool.

(1) The menu is only a minimally important cost-control tool.

    A. True
    B. False

(2) A menu can be designed to influence:

    A. The restaurant's location
    B. The amount a customer spends
    C. The price-reflective value assumption

(3) Product and worker flow in the kitchen is driven largely by:

    A. The menu-sales mix
    B. The appetizer and dessert selection
    C. The entrée-prep schedule

(4) A properly designed menu can direct the attention of the diner to:

    A. The best table in the house
    B. Specific menu items
    C. All menu items

(5) Cost control requires that only monthly inventories be taken.

    A. True
    B. False

ANSWERS: 1: B, 2: B, 3: A, 4: B, 5: B

Menu-sales analysis is a key element of any cost-control program

MENU-SALES ANALYSIS is absolutely necessary to understand how the sale of individual menu items affects your food cost, average check, and gross profit. The goal of menu-sales analysis is to identify those menu items that contribute the most — and least — to achieving your target check average, standard food cost, and profit goals. Once those items have been identified, appropriate action is taken to either sustain, improve, or decrease their respective impact on sales, costs, and profits through the design and layout of your printed menu.

The sales mix of menu items directly influences the overall food cost and sales volume, and each menu item impacts the overall average differently. Without the information provided by menu-sales analysis to analyze cost data, it is exceedingly difficult to isolate the real reason for a variance in cost standards. While a variance may result from a failure to follow standardized recipes or portioning, it also could stem from a shift in sales preferences to a higher-cost menu item or an increase in sales by meal periods. Menu-sales analysis will help you discover the reason.

Keeping track of the popularity of menu items is helpful in a number of ways. Sales records are utilized to help forecast future sales based on customer counts. Armed with such information, management is able to schedule employees, order food, and establish preparation quantities. With improved accuracy of forecasts, management can minimize overstaffing, eliminate excess inventory, and reduce leftovers and curb food waste.

The identification of popular and unpopular sellers will assist management in revising its menu. In fact, certain sales-analysis methods (described in *25 Keys to Profitable Success: Menu Pricing.*) actually will indicate what form your strategy should take with regard to such decisions as menu-item elimination, repositioning, pricing, and others.

18

Food cost must be analyzed from four dimensions or faces: maximum allowable, actual, potential, and standard

FOOD COST IS NOT A SINGLE-DIMENSION number or ratio. Food-cost percentage is sometimes misused and its importance can be both under- and overstated. Calculating a monthly food cost is relatively meaningless if it is not compared with a cost standard. In turn, the cost standard will have no real value unless it has been objectively determined. You cannot use another's food cost or apply a broad industry average.

In order to understand and appreciate just how relevant food-cost percentage is to the financial results, one must approach food cost from four different perspectives. In the first and most fundamental perspective, food cost is expressed as a percentage of total food sales. That percentage is calculated by dividing the food expense by the food revenue and is determined for individual menu items and for the total monthly food cost.

"Ideas won't work unless you do."

— ANONYMOUS

This is the "raw food cost" of preparing the item, and it is calculated from the standardized recipe, which follows purchase and portioning specifications. The accuracy and consistency of the cost calculations are directly proportional to how closely employees and management adhere to the specifications. Remember: Other factors can be altered that will change the food cost of any given menu item. They are as follows:

(1) The as-purchased prices of the ingredients (quality).
(2) The portion size (quantity).
(3) The menu price.

Maximum allowable food cost, or MFC, answers the question, "What food-cost percentage do I need to achieve my minimum-profit objectives?" Each restaurant will have a unique MFC resulting from different overhead expenses, depreciation schedules, labor costs, taxes, and insurance. The financial idiosyncrasies will determine the highest point food cost can rise and still achieve the minimum profit objectives. Therefore, MFC represents the "high-water mark" of food cost. If actual food cost exceeds that percentage, less profit will be earned; conversely, if it is lower, additional profit will be gained.

The second food-cost percentage, actual food cost, or AFC, is the default food-cost percentage reported on most monthly income statements. The food-cost figure is divided by the total food sales. If the operation follows the *Uniform System of Accounts for Restaurants*, the percentage will be the cost of food sold. However, it is more likely to be the cost of food consumed. The deciding factor is whether employee meals have been deducted. If employee meals are included, it is cost of food "consumed." An actual fiscal inventory must be taken as well. The AFC will typically be three or four points lower than the MFC, and it only tells management what the food cost is currently running. That is of nominal value unless the operator knows what the food cost should be running.

The third food-cost percentage, known as potential food cost — sometimes referred to as "theoretical food cost" — provides management with a qualitative percentage to compare against the AFC. The PFC is calculated by dividing the total weighted food cost by the weighted food sales. To arrive at the weighted food cost, the menu-item food cost from the standardized recipe is multiplied by the number sold of each respective menu item. All item food-cost totals are summed, and that becomes the total weighted food cost. That figure is divided by the total weighted food sales, which is arrived at by multiplying the number sold by an item's menu price. The sum of each menu item sales gives you the total weighted sales for the sales mix.

The resulting percentage is the PFC, which is the lowest figure that food cost can be because it assumes that there is zero waste and the full menu price was received for each item sold. It is a theoretical percentage in that it cannot be achieved because there will be some waste because of mistakes or quality-control losses. In addition, portioning is rarely perfect, and purchase prices may increase unexpectedly. Consequently, PFC must be adjusted to be a realistic figure that can be used by management.

The fourth and final food cost percentage, standard food cost, addresses those concerns by adding tolerances to the PFC for unavoidable waste, complimentary meals, employee meals, and all other foods consumed but not sold. That includes discounted meals and food transfers to the bar.

Total or weighted gross-profit return from a menu item is more relevant than the individual gross profit of any item

EVER SINCE THE INTRODUCTION of menu engineering, there has been, in my opinion, an over-emphasis on the importance placed on the individual gross-profit return produced by the sale of a single menu item. (Note: The alternative term for gross profit is "contribution margin.") Advocates of the gross-profit approach completely ignore food-cost percentage in their evaluation of menu items. The individual gross profit is the amount remaining to cover fixed costs and return a profit after food cost has been deducted from the selling price. For example, a steak dinner with accompaniments costing $7.25 and selling for $15.95 would return an individual gross profit of $8.70. This results in a food cost of 45.45 percent, which would be considered on the high side in most operations.

> **"Management's job is to see the company not as it is, but as it can become."**
>
> — JOHN W. TEETS

Menu engineering views a high gross profit and low food-cost percentage as mutually exclusive. Neither extreme is a correct or a sound perspective for analyzing your menu sales mix. Treating food-cost percentage and gross profit that way does not necessarily mean that additional dollars will flow to the bottom line. A number of things need to fall into place for that to occur. In some cases where high gross-profit items are emphasized at the expense of those with a low food cost, the actual gross-profit return per dollar of food cost is less than the return on sales mixes with lower gross profit and food cost. In addition, the gross-profit approach requires more sales to increase the bottom line.

Whenever demand is price inelastic, the gross-profit approach works well — for example, in country clubs, destination restaurants, and resorts. But price inelasticity is rare in competitive markets. Therefore, we need to look beyond the individual gross-profit return to the total or weighted gross-profit return realized from the sale of a menu item. An item with a high gross profit, such as the steak example cited earlier, may not be so popular as a pasta and vegetable dish that sells for $8.25 on a food cost of $2.85. Now suppose that one night you sell 20 pasta and vegetable dishes and four steak dinners. The total gross profit return is $108 and $34.80, respectively.

Obviously, you will put more dollars into your register and toward the bottom line with a popular menu item with a low-to-moderate gross profit than you will with an unpopular item with a high individual gross profit.

(1) Whenever demand is price inelastic, the gross-profit approach works:

    A. Well
    B. Only with take-out orders
    C. As a margin-cutter

(2) Menu engineering views a high gross profit and low food-cost percentage as mutually:

    A. Beneficial
    B. Symbiotic
    C. Exclusive

(3) An alternate term for gross profit is:

    A. Earnings before income taxes and depreciation allowance
    B. Contribution margin
    C. Income from operations

(4) Price inelasticity is common in competitive markets.

    A. True
    B. False

(5) MFC stands for:

    A. Maximum allowable food cost
    B. Minimum food controls
    C. Market forecast costs

ANSWERS: 1:A, 2:C, 3:B, 4:B, 5:A.

20

Your monthly income statement needs to be more than just an IRS form for determining tax liability

MANY OPERATORS DON'T QUESTION the format used by their accountant on their monthly income statement. Ask yourself, "Is my income statement a tool that helps me assess what is going on in my operation, or is it just a standard accounting statement?" If it is not really much help to you in evaluating operating costs, get a copy of the *Uniform System of Accounts for Restaurants*, seventh edition, from the National Restaurant Association.

The standard accounting format for reporting income and expenses is far too general to serve as an effective financial tool for management. While the income statement provides summary financial information — totals of income and expense during a particular accounting period — it can become a useful management tool with the addition of what I

> **"Sometimes it is better to do less and do it with commitment than to rush to complete a project."**
>
> — S. TRUETT CATHY

---

call managerial accounting information.

The income statement needs to include information that will allow management to assess specific aspects and areas of operations. Since financial statements are typically prepared just once a month, management probably relies on daily and weekly internal operating reports that supplement financial data with nonfinancial statistics, such as customer counts, labor hours, and menu sales. That kind of information is required to pinpoint variances and compare results with cost standards and budgets.

The information provided by the income statement can be improved greatly by separating sales figures rather than combining them. For example, if food sales comprise dining room, banquets, carry-out, and catered events, each should be shown separately. Alcoholic beverage sales should be broken down into beer, wine, and spirits. In addition, labor costs should be reported separately as hourly and management, restaurant and banquets, kitchen and bar, etc. That kind of detail is absent from most accounting income statements.

Expenses should be similarly separated by cost centers. Group expenses so they can be directly attributed to the revenues they produce. Separate fixed and noncontrollable expenses from direct operating expenses.

Each expense item should be expressed as a percentage of sales as well as its total dollar amount. Comparisons with historical figures for the same period provide value to the statement. Expressing each expense on a cost-per-cover basis provides even more information that adds to the interpretative value of the statement format. When standard accounting information is combined with certain nonfinancial data on the income statement, it becomes more valuable as a management tool.

(1) Financial documents like income statements are typically prepared:
   A. Once a year
   B. Once a month
   C. One a quarter

(2) The information provided by an income statement can be improved greatly by:
   A. Separating sales figures
   B. Combining sales figures
   C. Averaging sales figures

(3) Grouping expenses so they can be attributed directly to the revenues they produce:
   A. Is a good analytical tool
   B. Is misleading in terms of gross margin
   C. Is misleading in terms of net margin

(4) Never compare historical figures for the same period.
   A. True
   B. False

(5) You should separate fixed and noncontrollable expenses from direct operating expenses.
   A. True
   B. False

ANSWERS: 1: B, 2: A, 3: A., 4: B, 5: A

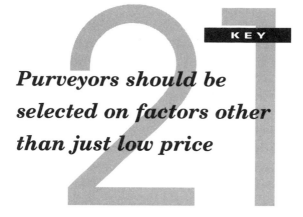

Purveyors should be selected on factors other than just low price

PRICE IS NOT THE MOST IMPORTANT factor when it comes to selecting a purveyor. Remember: Purveyors need to turn a profit if they're going to be able to serve your operation. The relationship between restaurant operator and purveyor must be mutually beneficial, or it will not work.

Nevertheless, price remains a consideration that can often make or break a sale. Consider this hypothetical situation: A meeting planner calls your restaurant to get a quote on a banquet. You quote a price, and the planner replies, "Our budget per person is lower than that. Can you give it to us for less?" If you quoted a price that you feel is fair, given your standards and financial considerations, you would likely be reluctant to offer a discount — even with the promise of future business. If no compromise is made, the meeting planner probably

> **"The bitterness of poor quality remains long after low pricing is forgotten!"**
>
> — LEON M. CAUTILLO

---

would find someone to supply the service at the budgeted price and end up regretting the decision. The disappointment of a bad meal lingers longer than the initial exhilaration of getting it at a low price.

Such is the case with suppliers. If you are a fickle buyer who is concerned only with purchasing at the lowest possible price, you will discover that the quality vendors will stop calling on you, while those that do will find a way to make a profit. You will also discover that the quality of the products you are using will be lower and that the level of service you receive will be directly proportional to how the purveyor values your business.

I remember a state restaurant association honoree who spoke to a roomful of students boasting how he regularly paid the lowest prices for everything he purchased. He explained that he had grown tired of dealing with individual salesmen, so he prepared a list of his weekly requirements and handed a copy to each sales representative who called on him every Monday morning. He went on to explain that he even let the reps meet together in one of his banquet rooms to fill out his bid sheets. After the reps had priced out his order, he collected the sheets and purchased each item from the supplier who offered the lowest price. Sound like a good idea to you? Although that restaurateur may have been paying the lowest prices offered by those who bid for his business, he was most likely not getting the best prices nor the best-quality products.

Many other factors contribute to the decision to pay a higher price for the same product. If all things were equal — product quality, reliability and reputation, delivery policies, credit policies, minimum-order quantities, days of delivery, etc. — then and only then would price be the basis for selecting one supplier over another.

(1) Price is really the only factor to consider when selecting a purveyor.

    A. True
    B. False

(2) The relationship between restaurant operator and purveyor must be mutually:

    A. Exclusive
    B. Beneficial
    C. Accredited

(3) Price considerations can often make or break a sale.

    A. True
    B. False

(4) The term "purveyor" refers to:

    A. An owner
    B. A customer
    C. A vendor

(5) Factors that contribute to a decision to pay a higher price may include:

    A. A purveyor's delivery policy
    B. A purveyor's reputation
    C. A purveyor's credit policy
    D. All of the above
    E. None of the above

ANSWERS: 1: B, 2: B, 3: A, 4: C, 5: D

22

Having to incorporate unplanned leftovers into production will raise your food cost and limit your menu-planning flexibility

LET ME BEGIN BY DEFINING what I consider to be a true leftover. A leftover is a food item that cannot be sold the next day in the same form for which it was originally intended. If it does not have to be altered in any way and can be sold at its regular price, it is not a leftover. No respectable, quality-oriented restaurant would attempt to pass off leftover baked potatoes as fresh the next day. They could be used to make hash browns, Lyonnaise, twice-baked, added to soup or made into potato salad. But in each of those cases, additional time and ingredients are required to transform them into salable menu items. And in almost all instances, the sales return will be less than what it would have been had they been sold as regular baked potatoes, thus increasing food cost.

In addition to having a negative impact on

food cost, the incorporation of leftovers can alter an operation's menu balance by sidelining the original vegetable or accompaniment. Incorporating leftovers assumes that your menu allows you to add daily specials and that you have a kitchen staff that is capable of preparing them. However, in both cases, the uncertainty of having 20 or 40 leftover baked potatoes will affect the quantity you must prepare. More important, how much would you prepare if you started from scratch? In addition, having an aversion to throwing anything away that is still edible may cause your standardized recipes to be violated. Extra ingredients normally not called for in recipes can result in increased food cost. Furthermore, customers may complain about the inconsistency in the contents of their soup or side dish.

Most restaurants today have a static menu — in other words, a menu that does not change from day to day. Therefore, they do not have an outlet for leftovers. Their menu items and cooking methods are designed to eliminate leftovers. The easiest way to accomplish that is to cook to order or cook in small batches. You should never end up with 20 leftover baked potatoes in the first place if you know your business. You do not put a full pan into the oven late in the evening; you put in only a half pan. With the advent of high-tech cooking equipment, we can recover quickly if we run out of an item. However, maintaining sales histories improves our forecasting to less than a 5-percent error rate. And we can throw away three or four potatoes without hurting our food cost and profit.

23

Cost controls alone will not ensure financial success

COST CONTROLS ARE JUST ONE important component of the overall business strategy. While statistics will demonstrate that many restaurants fail because the operator did not contain costs, adequate cost controls by themselves are no guarantee of financial success. You can't continue to reduce costs and grow. No business can cut its way to success.

When I see a chain restaurant — particularly those featuring hamburgers, pizza, or chicken — close one of its locations, I know it's not due to management's inability to control operating costs. Most of the national chains have sophisticated systems for monitoring costs. The more likely reason for closing is that the unit simply does not generate enough sales to return the desired profit.

The success of a business today is judged

by the TOP line, not just the bottom line. Raising profit margins on a flat sales base is not acceptable; it must be accompanied by growth, which requires new products, new customers, new relationships, and new services. The loss of customer confidence because of increased competition, ineffective management, poor food quality, and poor service cannot be overcome by cost controls alone. Once costs are controlled other strategies must be employed to increase sales and profit. Remember: Volume hides a multitude of cost-control sins. A unit with a low sales-volume notices every dollar of waste and labor inefficiency. If your entire focus is on cost control, you're ignoring the other critical aspects of financial success, like customer service, marketing, worker productivity, and job satisfaction. Consequently, cost controls should be just one aspect of your overall strategic business plan.

Cost controls are for maximizing profit, not minimizing losses

THIS SEEMINGLY SUBTLE DISTINCTION is critically important because maximizing profit and minimizing losses approach cost control from different perspectives. The way one goes about maximizing profits is considerably different from attempting to minimize losses. The former reflects a proactive, forward-looking, preventative approach, while the latter implies a strategy or plan of action taken once losses have been detected. Clearly, cost control requires elements of both. But if more attention is paid to maximizing profits, then less time will be required to take corrective action to minimize losses.

What would you think of a person who asked you to invest in his business after informing you how he was going to be extremely effective in minimizing your losses? I don't imagine you would want to invest in something like that unless you were seeking tax write-offs. And since the tax laws no longer favor tax shelter investments, only income-producing ventures are worth our money. But change that approach to something like "Let me tell you how I'm going to be able to maximize the profits of this venture," and you can see immediately how that positive perspective is far more inviting than the former.

As a professor, I have been challenged by students over the years who every once in a while will cite an example of a successful independent restaurant in which the owner-manager survived without most of the cost controls I lecture about in class. I recall one student who told me, "Garcia's doesn't have an inventory-control system, and they have been in business for over 30 years." I responded that it's true that some restaurants will be financially successful without practicing cost controls. However, they will never know how much more profit they could have made if they had practiced cost control.

Having a cost-control program in place during the good years will maximize the profit on each dollar sale. Cost controls are not something you turn to when losses are being incurred and financial ruin is at your door. You will operate longer, make more money, and be more successful than your competitors who do not practice some form of cost control. You will have a lower break-even point and earn a higher profit return on each dollar of sales. That is maximizing profit!

Operators who were not financially successful never planned to fail; however, they may have failed to plan

SEVERAL YEARS AGO at the National Restaurant Show in Chicago, I had the opportunity to listen to a presentation by Richard Melman, founder and president of Lettuce Entertain You Enterprises. His restaurants are among the most unique and creative concepts around. And most of the concepts he opens are financially successful. When asked about his success rate, he told the audience that the financial success of a concept mainly depends on what you do before you open the doors to the general public.

The failure rate of restaurants is one of the highest in the retail business. Some estimates cite a 60-percent failure rate within the first five years, with one in four operations never seeing their first anniversary. The 1990s has been called the toughest competitive market in the history of the industry. When you consider that several of the most successful chains have shuttered concepts nationwide, failure is not confined to the independent operator. In spite of all their deep financial pockets, management resources, and the latest electronic systems, chains cannot guarantee success.

For every corporate concept that fails — Darden Restaurants' China Coast, Brinker International's Grady's American Grill, Apple South's Tomato Rumba's, and PepsiCo's Hot 'n Now — hundreds of independent operations fail every day. I know how hard it is for an independent to survive in a climate of increasing governmental regulation, intensifying competition, critical customers, and shrinking labor pools because I've "been there, done that."

I don't believe that anyone would invest their time and money in a restaurant concept if he or she didn't truly believe that it would be successful. Entrepreneurs are risk-takers. The more knowledge and experience you have, the more you understand what it takes to be successful. Experience is a great teacher, and we often learn more from our mistakes than we do from our successes.

My stepfather entered the restaurant business at a time when, as he put it, "we could proceed with a trial-and-error decision-making." By the time he closed his last restaurant in 1974, he knew that trial-and-error was no longer allowed. In fact, one mistake would cost you more than you could ever expect to recover. The chain restaurants were entering his market, and as each one opened, he saw his business erode.

He said that if he were opening up for the first time in the mid-1970s, he never would have lasted as long as he did. His restaurants operated for 25 years. My restaurant lasted 11 years and closed in 1984. We were proud to know we lasted that long going up against the national chains.

Today, the independent operator needs more than financial backing to remain in business. You need to have a business plan. Many of the things that bring financial ruin to a businessperson — recession, inflation, low unemployment, high unemployment, interest rates, and tax laws — are not under his or her direct control. Such things must be endured. Cost controls are our means of defense and protection. We need to remove as much of the risk of failure as possible before we invest our time and money.

While preplanning is critical, it does not stop once your business is up and running. Cost control is not a one-time program or a pre-opening exercise; it is ongoing and present throughout the life of the business. If you do not have a cost-control system, you are vulnerable to the competitors who do. Planning is a strategy employed by professional restaurant operators, and cost controls are for *knowing where you're going, not for discovering where you've been.*

DAVE PAVESIC is a former restaurateur who now teaches hospitality administration at the university level. He previously owned and operated two casual-theme Italian restaurants in Orlando, Fla.; served as general manager of operations of a six-unit regional chain in the Midwest, operating four coffee shops, a fine-dining seafood restaurant and one drive-in; and was a college foodservice director. He currently teaches courses on restaurant cost control, financial management, and food production in the Cecil B. Day School of Hospitality Administration at Georgia State University in Atlanta, Ga. He has written numerous articles on menu-sales analysis, labor cost, menu pricing and equipment layout. His two other books are *The Fundamental Principles of Restaurant Cost Control*, Prentice Hall Publishers, 1998, ISBN 0-13-747999-9 and *Menu Pricing and Strategy*, fourth edition, Van Nostrand Reinhold Publishers, 1996, ISBN 0-471-28747-4.